GW00854627

Duncan Peter

DAILY ACTS OF CONSCIOUSNESS

FINDING MEANING IN THE MUNDANE

OMA, Thanks for your inspiration and example!

Table of Contents

INTRODUCTION

Some years ago, I got together with a group of friends and started a study group that we named: 'Making Sense of Metaphysics'. All of us were keen on self-development and spirituality and wanted to put what we understood in theory into practice.

For us, an intellectual grasp of metaphysics was not enough. We wanted to see how spirituality could impact our everyday lives. We had all experienced moments of incredible peace and joy, moments when we were very much in control of our inner lives and the world behind our eyes.

But, after we had meditated and enjoyed the great peace, we would go out into the world, and in no time, that wonderful state would be lost. We'd have to face the challenge of daily life, work, and relationships once again.

For example, as a team leader at work, I have to deal with difficult members of staff. John argued about any work given to him. Everything had to be explained in great detail before he would agree to do it. There were other colleagues who also presented different challenges. My social life had its own challenges. There was my forgetful friend, Miriam, who would often show up late or go to the wrong venue. Then, there was

Daniel, Mr Sulky, who continuously criticised everybody and everything.

So, the tranquillity and peace we had experienced while meditating, was lost once we opened our eyes to face the world. We all had challenging people in our lives.

However we all wanted our daily lives to reflect some degree of the consciousness we had attained in meditation. Only then would we feel satisfied that we were growing and evolving. One day, we hit upon the idea of a special daily practice that would enable us to see our progress.

Right from the start, before we began this daily practice, we agreed to acknowledge several 'Cosmic Givens'. These are the laws of the universe that come into play when we incarnate in a body and come to Earth. All of us recognised them as crucial and kept them in mind as we practised our daily routine.

COSMIC GIVENS

1. Planet Earth is a School

Yes, we are enrolled in a school. We are spiritual beings here to learn how to work with matter, how to materialise spirit and how to spiritualise matter. This is not as strange as it sounds. The more we practise, the clearer it becomes. We experience more and more of Nature's intelligence, bounty, and sense of order. It's as if when we accept that we are here to learn, life becomes an adventure, and different scenarios become opportunities to facilitate our growth.

2. Personality and Higher Self

When we are born, we have specific physical, mental-emotional characteristics that influence our behaviour and experiences. This is our personality. The personality is rather like the masks ancient Greek actors wore to represent their characters. Our personality usually manifests the ego-- driven side of our character. It is the part of us that wants to impress and prove our worth. However, we also have a higher self that behaves in a generous, kind and loving way. It is the spark of perfection that signals our connection to all living beings. Life on Earth tends to centre around our personalities. From a young age our personalities are protected and encouraged by the people around us. We are programmed to be the centre of attention and to impress with our charm and intelligence.

Too often, we identify so much with our personality and ego-self that we rarely contact the higher self, but the moments when we do are memorable and fulfilling. When we find that we are expressing more joy and peace, this indicates that we are displaying more of the higher self than the personality. Like the ancient actors with their masks, our higher self manifests through the personality, the mask that we use on Earth. Spiritual masters are a good example of how to use the personality to manifest the higher self. They allow their higher self to influence their thoughts, feelings, and actions or their personality.

This isn't always easy. The demands of our egos can trick us into forgetting that we have a source of wisdom that can advise and support us.

3. Cause and Effect

The law of cause and effect is fundamental to life on Earth. We cannot escape it. Our thoughts, emotions and actions resonate and impact our lives. Everything is recorded within. Anyone who has had a near death experience will verify this. They will confirm that the moment in which they were suspended between worlds, they saw past events from their life flashing before their eyes. Esoteric teachings explain that we will all watch 'the movie of our lives' with our helpers and guides when we go to the next world. We will see what we did well and where we could have done better. This informs our next incarnation on Earth and has an influence on how and where we incarnate.

We can see how our thoughts influence our emotions and eventually our actions. So if you want to verify it for yourself, you might like to do the following: think of three positive things that you are thankful for in your life. It could be to do with your home, job or relationships.

Once you start to think about them, you will find that you automatically think of related positive events. Now, you are on the 'thankfulness wavelength.' Being grateful and positive will link your thoughts to other times you felt this way energetically. However, the same also happens when you think of a negative experience. Perhaps you are disappointed because you missed a promotion at work; the more you dwell on it, the more you will remember other similar disappointments and, after a while, you will end up feeling quite glum and demoralised.

4. Reincarnation

Hindus, Buddhists, early Christians and even Pythagoras all promoted the doctrine of reincarnation. When Jesus restored the blind man's sight, his disciples asked him, "Who has sinned?" In other words was it his or his parents' karma that he was born this way? According to ancient teachings, we are born with the qualities that we developed in the past. These gifts and problems influence the direction of our current life. We continue to return to Earth in different situations, as different personalities, until we have learned all our lessons and paid off any debts.

Our future development can continue on other planets and in other dimensions, or we might choose to maintain links with the Earth and help others in their evolution.

The huge challenge that we all face is learning how to deal with the density of earthly vibrations. This pull of gravity restricts our sense of spirit. We suffer a kind of amnesia. We forget that there is more to us than just the ego or personality self.

Luckily, we get more than one attempt to master matter!

We return to Earth in different forms: male, female different races. With each incarnation, we hopefully expand our consciousness.

Those more evolved human beings have returned to Earth so many times and have learned so much about cosmic law that early on even in childhood, they are able to sense their spirit and higher self and walk the spiritual path without getting too distracted by the demands of the personality.

5. We Are Constantly Broadcasting

We are energetic beings, interconnected by a field of energy, according to quantum physics. Our life experiences are informed by how we look at the world and the ways in which we interact with it.

As within, so without: our inner state of being is constantly radiating out into the world. Like radios, we are receivers as well as broadcasters. We are receptive to other people's energy- usually subconsciously and, at the same time, we are constantly broadcasting our thoughts, emotions, and beliefs to others.

Sometimes, we might meet someone for the first time and feel uncomfortable with them. It is nothing to do with what they have done or said, it is just an irrational sense we have about them.

So, we avoid them. But could we be sensing their invisible energy? They may be going through a tough time and are putting on a happy face, but we can sense that something is not right.

Our big lesson is to be more aware of what we are broadcasting. Our task is to bring the qualities of the spirit— peace, joy, kindness, and, love into the physical world, and to give the spirit the right conditions to manifest.

When we are able to saturate and permeate our world with spirit, we experience joy and bliss. Not everyone calls it 'spirit.' It might just be a sense of fulfilment or expansiveness from doing something creative or charitable. It's that sense of wellbeing, of wanting to help and communicate without expecting anything in return, which shows that our actions are altruistic and stamped with the seal of spirit.

6. Our Cells Are Watching

We are carrying a community of trillions of cells in our bodies. These intelligent beings work hard to keep us healthy, and they all have their unique roles. The cells in the liver conduct different tasks from those in the heart. The cells in the different organs all work for the good of the whole. The moment they stop working harmoniously is when illness and disease take hold.

It became clear to our team, that if we want to have a consistent encounter with our spiritual selves, if we genuinely want to manifest harmony and peace in the world, then we must make sure to convince all of our cells, right down to the ones in our feet, to get involved.

A sage once opened a whole new world for me when he described cells as being like children. He meant that they are highly suggestible and take their cues from the being they inhabit i.e. you and me. When we show them a good example, they 'copy' our behaviour and are much more amenable to helping us on our path.

Modern research finds that attitude and state of mind have a definite impact on health. Advances in technology have only confirmed what the ancients knew intuitively.

Daily Experiment

My group of friends decided that some of us would do experiments and then feedback the results. We created an assignment for each day: a daily task that would inform our actions at **every moment** of the day. This is easier said than done of course!

Life is constantly presenting challenges. We found that, in the beginning, it was difficult to remember our practice for the day. Something would inevitably come up and we would be preoccupied with other things. This forgetfulness happened so frequently, that we had to set up phone calls to remind each other.

So, we created a 30 day plan of action, an assignment that encouraged us to fill the day with the vibes of the "spirit." It eventually became a pleasure and one which became addictive. The results were life-changing. My concentration levels skyrocketed, and my moods didn't fluctuate as much. On the odd occasion I lost impetus, I was able to perk up and remember the exercise, and how I had to report back to the others.

Interconnectedness in the Field

Synchronicity started to become more commonplace, after we had been doing the daily tasks for a few weeks. We would 'bump' into friends and colleagues that we had not arranged to meet. Just when we needed it, pertinent information would "mysteriously" answer a question we had, by coming up on the radio, TV or online. We would all experience seeing a billboard or an ad that was the answer to a question we had previously wrestled with.

The impact on my life was so huge that I repeated the 30 day plan the following month, and the next. Even now, I still go back to it, years later.

The assignments are multi-layered. As our consciousness expanded, we noticed that we would experience the same task differently, and that we would enjoy a deeper sense of fulfilment and a better understanding of life and the universe. Don't be fooled by the apparent simplicity of the tasks. They have levels and layers and can occupy us for years to come.

The Approach

Our other group of friends were impressed by our newfound serenity and cheerfulness. They were raring to go. They realised that, like us, they would need to give it time, and that they had to be consistent to reap the benefits. But they were prepared to be patient, and to collaborate with a partner to keep them on track.

Now, I suggest that the reader also works with a friend, just to keep you both on track. You can encourage one another when things get difficult. You are bound to have moments when you want to give up, but having a supportive person to confide in, will help to keep you committed.

The daily assignments have the potential to radically change consciousness. This has been the experience of everyone who follows the programme. I consistently found that if I practised the task for the day, it impacted my life in unexpected, positive ways.

We all come from different spiritual and psychological angles. We all favour one sense over others. Some of us are more visual, others more practical. Some want to be active, whereas others enjoy feeling emotions. All approaches are valid. We are bound to find some exercises more interesting than others, but, by practising them even when we aren't particularly keen to do so, we grow and develop into more rounded characters.

I found that the areas I most needed to work on were difficult to face when they appeared in the daily task. It is easy to 'zone out' when we come to a challenging daily task, but this is not the way to grow. If this happens to you, I suggest repeating the same task the following day, as it is likely to be an area that needs to be worked on.

Secrecy

Don't tell everybody that you are doing the 30-day programme; it only puts more pressure on you. This is where having a buddy who is also doing the programme is so useful. You can arrange a mutually convenient time to confide in each other on how you are getting on. This is a powerful way to learn, share and support each other.

You will find that once you get into the daily programme, people will notice that there is something different about you.

They might notice how well you look and ask if there's anything new going on in your life. This is proof, if you need it, that your inner work is impacting your outer demeanour.

Do the tasks in daily order if you can, but if you see a task ahead that you fancy doing, jump ahead by all means. What's important is to be consistent and to have fun doing the tasks. You can repeat them as many times as you like, it's up to you. The group kept records of the impact the tasks had on them, and you can read their **"Experience"** after the description of the daily task.

DAY 1:

MIDAS TOUCH

We leave traces on everything we touch. Vanga, a highly gifted clairvoyant, would hold an object belonging to her client, perhaps a ring or watch, and see their whole life: past, present, and future. Even the Bulgarian government consulted her at crucial times as her accuracy rate was said to be over 80 percent. In Western countries, the police will often consult a psychic if they need extra information about a crime. In doing so, they often receive new leads or confirmation of their suspicions.

So, wherever we go, wherever we walk or sit, we are leaving traces of ourselves. Have you ever gone into a room where a heated argument has taken place? Even if you were unaware that it happened, you can often sense the 'bad vibes' and you know something unpleasant happened.

This reminds me of the Greek myth of the greedy King Midas who asked the gods to give him the power to turn everything he touched, into gold. His wish was granted, but he soon found himself imprisoned by his greed and begged to go back to how things were before.

However, if we ask the invisible world to help us imbue everything we touch with golden **vibrations** of peace, light, and love, we will have a salutary effect on our world. At the same time, we will be working with our good selves: our higher selves.

TODAY'S TASK

Remind yourself to be more aware. Your feet are in contact with the earth. Everywhere you walk, feel a sense of peace, and broadcast it into the earth through your feet. Wherever you sit on the train, in the office, at home, be more aware that you are leaving an imprint. Leave the best one you can.

You may need to set an alarm to remind yourself to do this throughout the day.

EXPERIENCE

The day I started doing this, I found myself paying a lot more attention to my inner life. It did take a while to get into it, though. I found that I would be so busy doing other stuff that I'd forget to leave good traces. I tried to have the best thoughts and emotions, so that whatever I touched left calm, peaceful, and positive energy. I got so much out of it that I decided to do it again for several more days!(Ben)

DAY 2:

HARA – GROUNDING

The Japanese talk about having 'hara' or 'belly'. This refers to someone who is grounded, who isn't in their own head and lost in thoughts. My meditation group often discussed the issue of being too intellectual in our approach to change. We all felt too cerebral especially when trying new methods.

We regarded hara as essential for our spiritual growth. After all, we wanted to impact our spiritual life in a practical way.

I came across hara for the first time when learning Tai chi and chi gung. The teacher described a point, about an inch and a half to two inches below the navel, deep inside, past the skin. We were asked to work from this point. This was our centre.

When we think of this area, we realise how important it is. As a baby, we are nourished through the cord which is attached to us at the abdomen. After it is cut, we still have this potential link to the forces of nature.

Hara is where we feel and sense things. This is where we incarnate ideas and bring them to life. Through hara, we feel part of everything. There is a natural knowing in this centre. It may prewarn us of the presence of helpful or harmful forces.

TODAY'S TASK

Focus on your hara centre as you walk, talk and work. Feel your shoulders relax and let go. It will be as if you are allowing all of your energy to go down. If you have a problem to solve, try to 'feel' the ideas around the subject, as if you are thinking from inside your hara. Forget the mental gymnastics that we all go through. The hara is super intuitive and can lead us to an answer more quickly than the hours of analysing and pondering that we usually need.

EXPERIENCE

I suffered a lot from migraines, probably because I worried about things too much. When I started to put my focus on the hara, the migraines stopped. Being of a nervous disposition, I went through torture whenever I had to do a presentation at work. I wouldn't be able to sleep; my mind would constantly go through what I would say and the kinds of questions I might be asked. But when I started to rehearse my presentation with my focus on hara, it was a totally different experience. I felt supported and stable. My heart wasn't beating nineteen to the dozen. I now really enjoy doing presentations!(Lata)

DAY 3:

DEALING WITH DIFFICULT PEOPLE

I had good intentions. I was looking for happiness and peace of mind, but there was something that would irk me from time to time. It was as if I were being obstructed. Deep down I knew this was preventing me from enjoying a complete sense of fulfilment.

It was all well and good to touch everything with kindness and goodness, but now and then I would suddenly and unexpectedly think of someone who had been mean or who I did not get along with. My sense of wellbeing would change. My mood would shift. This was clearly not a healthy reaction.

However, when I found this specific form of meditation, things changed. I discovered the 'loving kindness approach'. It revolutionised my life. Dramatically! Much scientific research has been done on those who practise loving kindness meditation. The psychological and health impacts are measurable. (The brain changes, physical pain lessens, those who have suffered trauma are comforted This was enough for me to give it a go.)

After practising it for a while, I could not look at so-called enemies in the same way. The emotional charge was no longer there.

Even more surprising, I could not dislike them. It was as if loving kindness meditation gave me the ability to see things more holistically.

I personalised a lot less. I began to sense the relatedness of everything.

It was the Buddha who introduced his disciples to this meditation over 2000 years ago. Although I don't follow the exact wording used by Buddhists, I do think that we need to adapt it to our lives. It is the sense of friendliness and warmth that is important.

I guarantee that anyone who sits down and practises it seriously will eventually get such a great feeling that they will not want to miss a day. So here we go, put aside about 10 to 15 minutes for this.

TODAY'S TASK

Sit quietly and sense your breathing...

Now starting with your feet, send a feeling of thankfulness and friendliness to the cells there.

Smile at them. Gradually move up your body, to your calves, thighs, upper body, and head. Send feelings of gratefulness, kindness to all the cells, they work away, quietly in the background. Feel yourself letting go and relaxing. Thanking them for their work...

Next, bring to mind someone you feel a lot of affection for, send them this sense of friendliness, kindness, gratitude that they are in your life.

Then do the same for those you feel neutral towards, acquaintances, colleagues.

Once you have done that, think of people you have problems with: those you have had arguments with, or who you just don't get on with. Spend time sending them friendly vibes. Because you have been sending good feelings to the previous groups, you will now find it a little easier to extend this atmosphere of friendliness to them too.

Finally, do it universally. Send this sense of kindness to the universe, the stones, plants, animals, the stars and planets…..

EXPERIENCE

I was all set to do my loving kindness meditation. I sat down and began to make myself comfortable. Suddenly the doorbell rang. I was expecting a parcel, so I decided to answer the door. I was mortified to see a charity worker at the door, hoping to set me up with a direct debit. I was already donating money to that charity. I let him know in a very terse, tone. After all he had disturbed my loving kindness meditation, hadn't he? The irony of my response was not lost on me. I vowed not to let such things unbalance me in the future. Over time, I so enjoyed this approach that it became a habit. I felt this friendliness towards everyone. It became natural and spontaneous when I walked down the street or sat on a bus. Sure, from time-to-time, life would get tense, but those moments never lasted long.(Krystyna)

DAY 4:

STRANGERS BECOME FRIENDS

When we walk down the street in most countries in the West, we are careful to avoid eye contact with those we pass. It is thought of as either rude or threatening to look at people. This has created a society that is detached and cold. Many of us suffer from loneliness and isolation.

Yet, if we are looking to experience peace and joy, blanking other human beings is not conducive to expanding our awareness. Why? Quantum physics is increasingly realising, that we are all linked together on an energetic level.

We might like to think that we can be independent and do our own thing, but for real progress, we have to acknowledge that everything we think, feel, and do, impacts the world around us. This may not be immediately clear. However, in time, we realise that our actions eventually come home to roost.

TODAY'S TASK

As you walk down the street, when you go to the shops, wherever you are, send people good wishes. You don't need to say anything to them, or, stare at them, just know that you are wishing them well. True, many people look grumpy and preoccupied. We all have busy lives and a lot to think about. But if you decide to wish everybody well and hope that things will work out well for them today, I guarantee that you will feel incredibly good in yourself.

Do this without expecting a response. After all these are strangers who don't know you. See what happens.

EXPERIENCE

I did my best not to let my gaze stay on people for too long. As I walked to work, I spoke to passers-by in my head, making sure to feel what I was saying: "Good morning, have a great day" or "I wish you well", or "I hope your dreams come true". I came up with different wishes spontaneously, all positive and all heartfelt. Something began to happen. You know how most people have a fixed, hard expression when on their own? Strangely, I noticed that people I had sent a good wish to, seemed less tense and, their faces were growing softer. Some even smiled at me or said, "Good morning". These were people I did not know! Best of all, it put me in such a good mood because I could verify for myself that I was impacting other people.(Duncan)

DAY 5:

MATCHING FREQUENCY OF LIGHT

We all know the difference in our energy level when we are in a good mood. We feel light and easy, relaxed and expansive. However, when we have had bad news or feel grouchy, life becomes a strain. We tend to drag our feet. We walk with our heads down and, we feel constricted and constrained. We are plagued by the countless thoughts flitting in and out of our mind. We feel heavy. Gravity seems to be stronger than ever before.

Mystics throughout time have spoken about light. Not the regular light from the sun, but another kind of light. According to Genesis, the sun was created on the fourth day of creation, whereas the other light was there from the beginning: "Let there be light". Those were the first words to unleash creation.

This spiritual light has been experienced and seen by mystics. They describe it as permeating every part of the earth. We are in a sea of this invisible light. It interpenetrates all and is the source of creativity and spirituality.

As we got into these exercises, we all began to sense and see this light. A sudden burst would appear, unexpected and unannounced. It was confirmation that we were closing in on our Higher Selves.

When we fall in love, we are so joyful. Nothing gets us down. Problems are solved easily because we are in such a relaxed frame of mind. Wouldn't it be good if we could experience this lightness even if we haven't fallen in love? So today, let us make a concerted effort to consciously experience this lightness of being and remind ourselves to maintain it throughout the day.

This cosmic light is so powerful that we can surround ourselves and others with it. Essentially, we are light. By remembering this, we reinforce our true selves. If we are going through a bad patch with someone, the best thing to do is imagine us surrounded by cosmic light together. It reinforces their true self and ours too. Don't be surprised if things become less combative between the two of you, very quickly.

TODAY'S TASK

Before you go out, surround the place you are going to with light. Imagine this pure light filling your workplace or the shop you are going to. Send the light ahead of you and see what happens.

EXPERIENCE

The first time I practised this, I made a real attempt at feeling light and happy. I felt more whole when I immersed friends and difficult people in this light. It seemed to soften everything. My arthritis was less painful. I felt sustained and supported. It was as if I had a friend with me. I will definitely continue to do it. (Jane)

DAY 6:

PROGRAMMING THE UNIVERSE

The popularity of books such as "The Law of Attraction" confirms the instinct we all have to exert some kind of control over our lives. We all know that thoughts are powerful and so we want to be able to use them to create the life we desire.

As you get further into these daily exercises, you will find that strange things start to happen. You seem to be in the right place at the right time. It is as if the universe is looking out for you. It provides everything you need, but in its own time. Then, when you look back, you see that its timing is always perfect.

There is nothing wrong with attracting money into your life. Or you may want extraordinary health and beauty. The crux of the matter is that we must not exploit others to get what we want: there needs to be a sense of responsibility.

We are all interconnected on an invisible level, whether we realise it or not. It is wise to look at the ethics of the issue and how we can help others when we receive what we want. How can we help those less fortunate than ourselves when we attract money into our lives? Will our extraordinary health induce us to support those who are incapacitated and need errands run for them?

TODAY'S TASK

Spend some time in your imagination, and, create the kind of life situation you want. See yourself attaining whatever you want but also see yourself helping others with your achievements. If you do not have anything that you particularly want, then you can visualise qualities such as kindness and patience. Whatever takes your fancy.

EXPERIENCE

I had just returned to England after a 3-month stint doing charity work in Africa. Of course, I had to give up my previous job to go. So, when I got back, I was a little concerned about finding a new job, especially as we were in lockdown because of the pandemic. After being rejected for countless jobs and being unemployed for a few months, I decided to start visualising myself doing work that was good for the environment and of service to people. Some weeks after starting this, a family friend visited us. When he heard that I was looking for work, he mentioned that his company had a vacancy. I applied, passed the interview, and found myself employed!(Mary)

DAY 7:

GRATITUDE OPENS
DOORS TO HAPPINESS

Life can be tough. It can be fast, demanding, and disappointing. It's easy to forget that in spite of this, there is still a lot in our lives that we can be happy and grateful about. The exciting thing is that research has found that being grateful can improve health and change attitudes.

For example, a 2011 study published in *Applied Psychology: Health and Well-Being* found that if you spend 15 minutes writing down a few things that you are grateful for before going to bed, you may sleep better. Everyone knows how important sleep is for physical and mental health. Another study found that grateful people suffered fewer aches and pains. They tended to be less grouchy and more likely to look after themselves better, to exercise more, and to see their doctor less often.

TODAY'S TASK

The magic mantra for the day is "thank you". But don't just say it. Think about the things in your life that you are grateful for. It could be a loving partner, a job you love, caring parents, or good health. If we really scrutinise our lives, we are bound to find at least a few things to be grateful for. We may even be grateful for difficult events that happened in the past, people we met who have contributed to our growth.

Throughout the day, really focus on feeling grateful for the things that you have. It is so easy to take things for granted and to get lost in the hubbub of life. Practicing gratitude will probably mean that you start to slow down a little. It helps us get a better perspective on life.

EXPERIENCE

I am a bit of a worrier. I get lost in mental gyrations and what ifs. What if this doesn't happen or if that happens? Or if I do this and that happens? A constant barrage of questions and fears. Of course, most of my worries prove to be unfounded. But since I started practising gratitude and counting the good things in my life, I have been less tense and stressed. I have found that I have more time for others, and I am less self-fixated. Life has become more enjoyable. (Leo)

DAY 8:

YOU ARE HOW YOU EAT

Eating is very social. We eat with friends and family to catch up with them. By sharing a meal, we can pick up on how their day went and find out their latest news. When we meet up with friends that we haven't seen for a while, we enjoy a meal with them and find out what has been happening in their lives. When we celebrate, we eat and drink together. We are accustomed to eating with others.

However, it is important for us to eat on our own when we can. When we do so, we can experience a new sense of fulfilment. Eating alone and in silence, without any background sound, TV or radio, can trigger a huge sense of peace and wellbeing.

When we eat we are performing a kind of alchemy. The food we eat is imbued with our thoughts and feelings. Our consciousness, when eating, impacts our digestion and our mood.

Of course, when we eat with someone, we chat and converse. This makes it quite difficult to consciously extract the more subtle side of the food we eat. It is important not to eat when we are feeling angry, sad, or emotional in any way. Why? Because it will impact our digestion and perpetuate our mood. It can even make us ill. It is better to wait until we are calmer and less perturbed.

When we eat alone, we can concentrate on chewing our food: And when we do so, our saliva has chemical substances that enhance digestion.

As we open our mouths to eat, it can be a wonderful chance to practise meditation. So, for example if we are eating salad, we can think about the vegetables. We can imagine how they were planted and grew. Above all, by being thankful for the food, we can extract maximum goodness, which can only contribute to our emotional and physical health.

By eating mindfully, we might find that we feel fuller after eating less than normal. We feel full on less food without even trying! This is because we have extracted more of the goodness from the food, which is less likely to happen when we are chatting away.

Eating mindfully is another kind of meditation. If done properly, it has many of the benefits of mindfulness meditation. We are focussed on the moment, present and aware. You may find the benefits are so real that you become hooked on eating in silence. You might even convince friends and family to join in.

TODAY'S TASK

We eat in silence. We use our mind to envisage where the food was grown, how the sun shone on it, how water nourished it, how it was harvested. We involve our emotions, feelings of thankfulness and pleasure. By chewing carefully, we break down all the constituent parts of the food and provide our body with the nutrients it needs.

EXPERIENCE

Over the years I have become sensitive to certain foods. I tended to avoid them as they affected my digestion too much. When I started to eat in silence, as a kind of meditation, things began to change. I made sure to eat slowly and thoughtfully, really being in the moment. After eating in this way for a while, I was able to eat the foods that had disrupted my digestive system previously. Eating in silence has revolutionised my life. (Krish)

DAY 9:

THE POWER OF WORDS TO CHANGE THINGS

Unless we undertake a serious attempt to minimise the number of thoughts flitting through our heads, we will all have some kind of inner dialogue going on. What we say to ourselves is crucial. We can make or break our life or someone else's just through the words we utter.

Psychologists advise parents to be careful of the kinds of limitations they put on their children by careless talk. For example, we might get angry with a child and say something unkind. That can have a detrimental effect on their self-esteem and have ramifications through their adult life.

I remember at school we had a few pupils who obviously suffered because of withering put- downs at home. They were especially desperate for the teacher's attention. Luckily, we had some excellent teachers who went out of their way to encourage them. Hopefully all of the negative comments they received at home were neutralised by the teacher.

Similarly, if we have lots of negative words going around in our heads, we need to be like those teachers. We can change our inner landscape when we challenge diminishing self-talk and aim for a more positive inner dialogue.

Words have a power. Energetic power. Ancient civilisations were aware of this. Many had prayers, mantras and phrases that were seen to enhance wellbeing, and some were used to invoke protection or help.

It is really worth saying certain words out loud to see the impact they have. Words such as 'joy' 'peace' 'happiness' and 'love' or 'war' 'hate' 'enemy' and 'foe'. All these words not only convey a meaning, but also release energy in our lives.

In the book 'Words Can Change Your Brain', Dr Andrew Newberg, a neuroscientist and Mark Robert Waldman, a communications expert, show that "**a single word** has the power to influence the expression of genes that regulate physical and emotional stress".

When you say a word out loud, the sound vibrations have an impact on matter. Sound is made up of wave vibrations. Cutting edge research shows that sound creates patterns in our energy field. New scientific discoveries are confirming ancient wisdom!

TODAY'S TASK

Be particularly aware of how you talk to yourself. What kinds of words do you use? Do you tell yourself off or do you encourage and boost yourself? Spend time saying words out loud, such as 'harmony' and 'peace'. See what happens when you remember to repeat them throughout the day.

EXPERIENCE

I was a tense, nervous child, often gripped by worry and uncertainty. This meant that I took slightly longer than other kids to pick things up at school. I overheard my teacher say that I was 'slow' to another teacher when I was about 10. This only made me tenser and slower. In my later teens, I got a more realistic view of my abilities and that of others. I realised that I wasn't as 'slow' as some of my friends. I found some subjects easier than others. Once I reached adulthood, I wasn't totally confident. The 'slow' label haunted me. So I made up a phrase that I said to myself: "I understand things quickly and easily". Whenever I had an episode of feeling inadequate, I would repeat the phrase or a comparable word. By uttering the phrase and feeling what it was like to be confident, I would find that I was less perturbed and quicker to pick things up.(Krystyna)

DAY 10:

THE ANSWER LIES
IN THE FEET

The feet are our link with planet Earth. They ground us and stop us from becoming too spaced out. If you do find that you are too much in your head, massage your feet and see how it helps to bring you back down to earth!

Our task on Earth is to bring the qualities of our spirit down here. To bring harmony and peace into our everyday lives.

The Chinese include the feet in acupressure. They teach that all the organs of the body are reflected in the feet. Reflexologists work on the feet to enhance relaxation and reduce stress.

A friend who is a reflexologist told me about a time when she was with a client. She knew nothing about his health status, but as she worked on his feet, she sensed that all was not well in his lung area on one of his feet but not the other. When she mentioned this, her client confirmed that he only had one lung!

Who would have thought that the feet reflect our physical health? It is even more exciting to know that we can influence our health through the feet. For example, if you have a headache and are finding it hard to do anything, massage your toes gently. This can often ease the tension and pain.

TODAY'S TASK

A habit well worth getting into is washing your feet in warm/hot water every night before going to bed. Why? During the day, we are continually exchanging energy with the environment around us, both positive and negative. The feet pick up and expel energy. By washing them before going to bed, we stand a much better chance of having a good night's sleep and sweet dreams!

EXPERIENCE

My work is quite demanding. I am constantly in touch with people who have health problems, and many are seriously lacking in energy. By the end of the day, I am exhausted. I could not manage without taking care of my feet. I give them a whole lot of care before I go to bed. After washing, I gently massage and rub them. This makes a huge difference to how well I sleep: I have noticed that if I miss out on this ritual, I don't fall asleep as easily, and I wake up tired. (Duncan)

DAY 11:

THE HIDDEN ENERGY IN OUR HOMES

Everything is vibrating with energy, as we know. All our clothes, curtains and furniture are all vibrating energy. But what determines the quality of that energy? It depends on where the objects were previously. Who owned them? Are they new or second-hand?

Have we been through a particularly difficult time and is our house saturated with this past energy? This can have a definite impact. Our bed, settee, chairs, and utensils are all imbued with our energy. If we have a partner or flatmates, they also contribute their energy to the mix. We are constantly recycling the same old energy, unless we make a conscious effort to break the cycle.

All is not lost. There is a way of freshening and clearing the atmosphere and the vibrations. We will look at what we can do about it later.

Do you have 'second-hand' furniture? If you do, the previous owner will have left their vibes. They may be good, and that's great. But if they aren't, we must do something about it.

As we practice the daily recommendations in this book, we are on the way to reducing our subconscious, negative habits. This will inevitably lead to better, more pristine emanations from us into our home. So, we may end up working to neutralize the previous dingy, vibrations with robust, positive ones.

This is an exercise that will help: give yourself ten minutes on your own. If you have a partner or flatmates who want to participate, even better.

TODAY'S TASK

See your home in your mind's eye. Focus on its atmosphere. Feel and sense it. Now, visualise a bright sun above your home. This light is shining on the front, back and sides of your house. Allow the bright, radiant light of the sun to slowly descend through the top of the roof and gently permeate the upper floors. Gradually, let it make its way through the house to the ground floor. While it moves, it will collect any dingy, dull energy and takes it deep below the home into the earth. Here it is transmuted and cleansed. You can do this several times, until you feel satisfied that you have cleansed the house.

You are bound to have a new sense of lightness after doing this. Do the cleansing whenever you feel it is necessary. You are the best person to judge how frequently it needs to be done.

EXPERIENCE

When I moved house, I was given furniture by family and friends. It was my first property, and everyone was eager to help.

After a few weeks of living there, I noticed that I didn't feel too good. I felt lethargic and heavy and could not work out what it was. I was eventually drawn to a small dining table that the previous owner had left in the house. As soon as I got rid of it, I immediately noticed a huge difference. I also did the cleansing exercise, which also helped. What a relief!(Leo)

DAY 12:

YOUR AURA IS SHOWING!

All living things have an aura. Some auras are more complex than others. The human aura is highly complicated, with many nuances and subtleties. On average the aura is a three-foot electromagnetic field around the body. Kirlian photography can show some of the auric field.

Our thoughts, emotions and actions are reflected in the shapes and colours of our aura. We carry it around with us, and as we age it tends to fade and weaken.

Some people are born with the ability to see the aura, while others can train themselves to see it. In the past, before humanity started to develop their collective intellect, we were much more aware of the auric field. If you look at old paintings of the saints, they were invariably depicted with a golden halo around their head. This is what the artist saw. A golden aura denotes the transmutation of negativity and the development of wisdom. You could say that, in the past, this ability to perceive the auric field was more common.

Joseph's 'coat of many colours' is mentioned in the Bible. This is an allusion to his aura. He had developed so many qualities that they were apparent in his auric field in the plethora of colour there. Different virtues have vibrations that manifest as a specific colour in the auric field. Joseph's brothers tried to destroy the beauty of his 'coat', or his reputation, because he was his father's favourite son.

Our thoughts and emotions vibrate around us and are shown in our auric field. We may come across people, who, even though they are well- dressed, somehow exude an energy that makes us feel uncomfortable. We might try to avoid sitting next to them or even being in the same room as them. Others that we meet are different. We feel comfortable in their presence and often strike up a conversation with them easily in public.

Our true character is reflected in our aura. We cannot hide. We are continually broadcasting who we really are. It is not static: it changes with our mood and thought processes. But we can improve the quality of our aura. There are two ways we can work on it. First we can use our imagination and sensitivity and feel the colours change. We can visualise them getting clearer and more beautiful. However, this will not last forever. They will revert back to the original colours unless we also work on changing the qualities that led to that hue.

For example, if we are continually impatient and irritated— we are creating a reddish hue, but we can train ourselves to be calmer and less agitated. The calmer we become, the more blue we attract. So blue will begin to surround us, but If we don't continue to display this newfound patience in our lives, the blue will revert back to angry red!

TODAY'S TASK

Before you set off to work or when you are on the train or bus, be aware of the space around you. How does it feel? How far around you does it stretch? How far in front and behind? How far on the sides? Try and get a sense of it, its colour and its textures. Make time to visualise and **feel** the different colours. Look at a prism to get an accurate idea of the different colours.

What do the different colours stand for? Here is a very brief description of the colour meanings:

- **Red** - passion, courage, energy
- **Orange** - emotion, health, wellbeing
- **Yellow** - intellect, communication
- **Green** - balance, nature, optimism
- **Blue** - peace, truth
- **Indigo** - power, inner strength
- **Violet** - creativity, inspiration, spirituality

EXPERIENCE

Sometimes, I get so involved with my office work that I lose track of what is happening around me. Worse than that, I started to get terrible headaches a few months ago. When I sat down quieted myself and tuned in to the energy field around me, I found that there was not much energy in the bottom half of my aura. Most of my energy was around my head area. I started to do more breathing exercises and visualised the energy as an egg shape around my body, including the space below the feet. I also made sure to go for brisk walks each day. This did the trick for me. (Alex)

DAY 13:

MONA LISA SMILE

Walk down any busy street in the West these days, and you are going to notice many very rushed, tense, and glum looking people. We have allowed life to become so busy that we are mentally preoccupied most of the time. Life has become serious for sure. We have--- that report that must be done, then the appointment with the child's teacher, later we have to meet with the bank manager, and so the list goes on. Each day new things are added, and we feel more burdened. No wonder so many of us are suffering from burnout.

But we all carry a whole community within us, trillions of cells. They are our inner world. They provide structure in the body. They form tissue, which make up the organs in the body. Increasingly, research is beginning to acknowledge that the cells in our body are highly receptive to our inner state, to our consciousness. They experience our emotions and thoughts. They know us better than anyone else!

In healthy individuals, the cells all work together for the good of the whole body. However, sometimes things can become chaotic. The cells in one organ may not work in harmony with the rest of the body and this is when disease ensues.

Even though our cells are continually working to keep us well, there are times when they take their lead from us. If you are going through a particularly difficult time, it has an impact on your inner world. Harmony is disrupted and disorder reigns. The cells find it more difficult to complete their tasks and illness rears its ugly head.

Our cells are very much like children. They watch and imitate. If our outer life is a mess, if we attack others with our thoughts, if our emotions are all over the place, this influences how our cells 'behave'. So, if we want to be healthy and well, if we want to be in the right place at the right time, we have to become super vigilant.

TODAY'S TASK

Allocate some quiet time, preferably first thing in the morning. In your imagination, visit the cells in your feet. Consciously thank them for all their work, and **smile** at them. Wish them well. Continue to move up your legs, sending gratitude and warmth to the cells there. Continue in this way, working up the whole body, finishing at the top of your head.

EXPERIENCE

I suffer from a mild form of arthritis. My hands can be painful at times, but this pain is very much influenced by my state of mind. If something is stressing me out, my hands become slightly claw- like and ache. When I started to do the exercise, smiling, and wishing my cells well, starting from my feet I found that by the time I got to my hands, they were already less painful and less clenched. This has had such a noticeable impact, that I now do it every day without fail. (Duncan)

DAY 14:

GETTING RID OF INNER AND OUTER CLUTTER

Being surrounded by clutter can have a detrimental effect. The objects around us store energy which inevitably has an influence on us. They hold memories that may have a negative impact. There are many reasons why we hoard stuff. Sometimes we attach sentimental value to things. We may hold onto things because they were given to us by someone who is important to us. Other times, we feel like hoarding things because we are convinced that they may come in handy one day. There are so many reasons why we may feel moved to hold on to things. Certain things are useful to keep, but this is not the case with everything.

We all lead busy lives. It is so easy to allow stuff to build up and make our home look like a rubbish tip. I found myself in this situation a few years ago. I decided that I would get rid of all of my superfluous stuff. I had amassed lots that I did not use but felt compelled to keep-just in case!

Books are an addiction. I can't resist a new book by an author I like. I decided to go through my bookshelves and pull out all the books that I had finished reading and didn't want to keep. Believe me there were many. Almost half of my collection. I had either outgrown them, or the subject no longer interested me. I passed them on to charity shops or gave them away to friends.

Next I did the same to my wardrobe. Any clothes I no longer used were recycled. Unwanted objects, old vases, old curios and things I was keeping 'just in case' were recycled or passed on.

It felt so liberating. I'd previously wasted so much time looking for things because there was so much other stuff that I had to wade through to find it. It felt good.

TODAY'S TASK

It's not a good idea to spend hours decluttering. It can be exhausting. It is far easier and psychologically healthier to do, say, 15 minutes each day. Choose the most cluttered room in the house and work on it every day until you are satisfied. A little at a time is easier to handle.

EXPERIENCE

I didn't know what it was: I felt so tired all the time. I saw my doctor, and she did all the tests she could think of but found nothing. I finally concluded that my problem was an energetic one. I felt exhausted after getting home every day. The clutter that I had accumulated was immense. I had recently been through a divorce and so found it tough to finish work and come home and tidy. I just wanted to chill. But things couldn't go on as they were. I knew that I needed to make an effort to tidy up and declutter the house, so I started with a few minutes each day. If it could not be recycled, I threw it away. I was ruthless. I filled bags with rubbish. It revolutionised my life. It was exhilarating. I got my energy back. Coming home became a pleasure. I was able to unwind and do other stuff—play badminton and meet up with friends. I had a new zest for life. (David)

DAY 15:

MOTHER NATURE FOREST BATHING

How many times have you felt so exhausted with your personal problems that all you want is to go off for a walk in nature? Once you do, do you find that you have a whole new perspective on life? For a few moments, you can forget what's bugging you. Sometimes, just taking a break, helps us to come up with a solution.

The Japanese have done much research into what they call 'forest bathing' or 'shrinyin-yoku.' They have examined the benefits scientifically and know the advantages of a walk in nature. It can help us overcome health challenges. It reduces stress, lowers blood pressure, and enhances memory. Trees and plants emit a chemical called phytoncides, that boosts the immune system.

Of course, we all enjoy nature in our own ways. All our senses may come into play: the fresh smells, the birdsong, the strength of the trees when we lay our hands on them, the sheer beauty of the woods.

Doctors in Japan prescribe time in the woods to some of their patients and the impacts are being monitored with great interest in other countries. The more time we spend in front of screens, the less healthy we seem to be. This is especially true where children and teenagers are concerned. It could enhance their wellbeing if we encouraged them to spend time in nature from a young age. What a great habit this would be to take into adulthood!

I find that going into the woods slows my thinking down. I enter a more meditative space as I lose myself in the immensity and peacefulness of the forest. I often come away with new, creative ideas that enhance my personal and professional life.

Thoreau was aware of the benefits of being in nature. He said: 'We can never have enough of nature'. He did not need to see the scientific evidence. He just knew intuitively that it made him feel peaceful. It is said that he would spend hours each day, walking in wooded areas, soaking in the atmosphere.

Some of the recent evidence is quite staggering. Between 1972 and 1981, a Pennsylvanian hospital study found that patients whose beds faced trees, healed from surgery more quickly than those who faced a brick wall. It has also been found that adults who spend at least 30 minutes a week in a park, have lower blood pressure!

TODAY'S TASK

Make the decision to visit a park or forest, somewhere you can enjoy being amongst trees and shrubs. Plan to spend time in nature daily. It doesn't have to be for long periods. It may not always be possible to spare the time, but the impact on health is so enormous, that it is worth the effort.

Omraam Mikhael Aivanhov, a Bulgarian sage, has an amazing exercise for when we are out in nature. He says to pick the largest, healthiest- looking tree. Trees are reservoirs of energy from the sun and earth. They are living, intelligent beings. Recent research has even found that trees communicate with each other through their roots! So, once you choose your tree, ask it, if it would be kind enough to pass some of its strength on to you. Stand with your back against the trunk, your left palm held against your back and, your right palm on your solar plexus. Stay there for a while, feeling the energy working through your hands. When you feel recharged, thank the tree, and continue your walk.

EXPERIENCE

I've now got into the habit of spending time in nature whenever I can. I have seen the impact that it has. I am able to find solutions to problems and worries more easily. It is as if the quiet and peace of nature, allows me to access a knowing, creative part of myself. It took several visits to the forest before I was able to tap into my creativity and peace of mind, but it's definitely worth it!(Paul)

DAY 16:

FEELING BLUE?
GREEN WITH ENVY?
SEEING RED?

The impact that colour has on our psychological and spiritual lives is incredible. How dreary life would be without colour! Ask anyone who watched a black and white TV before colour sets became available, and they will tell you how it transformed their whole experience.

We all have a relationship with colour, and we are all influenced by it, whether we are conscious of this or not For example, psychologists know that when you sit in a room that is painted red, your blood pressure is likely to go up. And sitting in a blue room tends to lower it.

Advertisers spend a fortune making sure products are the right colour to boost sales and grab consumer interest. Packaging colour can make or break a product.

As we have seen previously, when we discussed the aura, colour is extremely revealing from a spiritual viewpoint. Each colour has a meaning. The colours that attract and repel us, are indicative of our state of mind, our aspirations, and our consciousness.

When we look at a rainbow, we see the visible spectrum of light. Red is at one end of the spectrum because, it vibrates more slowly than the violet ray, which is at the other end, the fastest frequency.

Our thoughts, emotions and actions all contribute to our vibratory frequency. When we are cheerful and happy, we are vibrating faster. It means that we are broadcasting 'good news' to our environment. As the law of correspondence dictates: 'as you sow, so shall you reap'. Our energy seeks out events that will reflect our positive state.

When we are most tired and worried, we vibrate more slowly. We are metaphorically dragging our feet and attracting less positive events into our lives. This is how we create our destiny.

The truth is that our emotions can fluctuate a lot in the course of a day. Some things make us feel good and others have the opposite effect. We are constantly broadcasting different energies which can send out confusing messages to the universe, this can account for the up and down nature of our life. If we want to attract a constant, balanced stream of positive events, we need to become more consistent in our vibrational state i.e. in our behaviour. This isn't always easy. After all we are constantly interacting with other human beings who unsettle us and influence our behaviour. It takes real discipline to stay on an even keel. It's hard but not impossible.

Colours have meaning and influence. We can heal ourselves, gain inspiration and develop positive qualities by working with colours. Each ray stands for its own strength or gift.

In esoteric spirituality, each ray comes under the influence of its own invisible entity. The rays are the abodes of advanced beings, who nourish the planet and exert a positive influence on us.

We can work with these rays by using our imagination and sensing how to incorporate their qualities, into our lives. On certain days you may have a lot of vim and vigour and are constantly on the go, which is the influence of red. Then you think that you may need to slow down and be less active, corresponding to blue. This can be achieved by breathing deeply and slowly and by being more sedentary.

Now, we can look at the qualities of each of the seven colours of the spectrum, noting which ones we like, and which ones we would prefer to avoid. Our goal is to balance all the colours so that we are able to call upon them as and when we need to.

RED RAY: This is practical and down to earth. The colour of passion, and practicality. 'Red blooded' and 'dynamic', are words that are often used to describe this first colour on the spectrum. It vibrates slower than the others, but it is the colour of courage and rage. The shade of ray determines which aspect you are manifesting. To get an accurate knowledge of each ray's hue, it is best to look through a prism.

We manifest the negative connotations of red when we are domineering and overpowering, but at its purest, red is excellent for developing will power. It gives us the will to get things done. Altruistic people who go out of their way to help the less fortunate, are examples of the positive manifestation of the red ray. They exert themselves for others.

ORANGE RAY: Orange is the colour of health and wellbeing. Made up of the will of red and the cheerfulness of yellow, orange creates an easy-going but strong willed person. Orange robes are often worn by Buddhist monks, to signify detachment, independence and compassion.

It is also the colour of digestion and nutrition. Fasting monks, find that wearing orange lessens cravings and feeds them on a more subtle, less physical level. The colour rules the stomach area.

Orange helps athletes and sportspeople to maintain their vitality and dynamism. It is different from the raw power of red. Orange is more disciplined and controlled but still open and accessible.

An 'orange person' is sociable and generally extroverted. Movement and dance are important to them, but if they can't move for health reasons, they are more than likely to enjoy watching sports and dance.

YELLOW RAY: Yellow stands for communication. It is the abode of intellectuals. The thinkers' colour, you could say. People who are comfortable with yellow are generally cheerful and exuberant. They are curious by nature and constantly asking questions. They like to know what makes others tick and they love to try to comprehend and work things out.

Their insatiable interest in the world, coupled with their ability to communicate, makes them good writers and journalists. Those working on this ray are generally good humoured and cheerful. However, to embody the negative side of yellow, is to be overcritical and sarcastic.

At its highest level, yellow turns to the gold of wisdom. Those channelling this wavelength understand the workings of the universe and the role humanity plays in the evolution of the planet. This is why artists in the past depicted a gold light above the heads of saints.

GREEN RAY: This is the centre of the colour spectrum. Green links to the heart and those who respond to this ray have an expansiveness about them. They are simultaneously kind and detached. Strongly linked to nature, you will find them retreating into woods or forests when they need to replenish themselves. Too much interaction with others can leave them exhausted. They enjoy being alone and soaking up Mother Nature's atmosphere.

They have times when they enjoy company but also times they prefer to be on their own. They are good family members. As parents they are extremely protective and supportive.

They have kind hearts and will go out of their way to help others. Often, they will volunteer to work for a charity. They make good healers, and their presence alone can be healing. Many attract the attention of others especially with their healing hands.

There is a quietness about them, and they are not generally overly chatty. Their skill is to sense and feel things out. They are very receptive to atmosphere and will make sure their home is peaceful. When they eat out, they are careful to choose a quiet place.

BLUE RAY: This is the home of the cool, calm and collected. Those who are 'blue' can come across as distant and cold. Like the blue sky which feels so far away, blue is at once detached and inclusive. When it is manifested in a negative way, blue is the colour of the depressive. This is when it's hard to do anything, and they simply don't have the energy to engage with the world.

However, it is also the ray of the communicator, but not in the way of the yellow ray. It is more measured and thoughtful. It is not over- communicative or a big fan of small talk. When it communicates, it is likely to say something important and worthwhile.

Silence is important to them. Many are drawn to religious institutions that are separate from society, and live monastic lives.

INDIGO RAY: Indigo is a combination of blue and purple. This ray is linked to intuition and the ability to sense the invisible. It is related to the third eye. Inner sight is most accurate when we are able to still our minds and focus on the subject at hand. Much like looking at a reflection in a pool of water, we can see the trees reflected only as long as the pool is still. If a stone is thrown into the pool the reflection is disrupted and disturbed.

There is an aura of mystery around indigo; people with this energy may come across as though they are holding something back. This may just be because they are receptive to the invisible and are trying to decipher what it is that they are seeing and sensing.

VIOLET RAY: This is the ray of spiritual power. It offers the ability to sense and go beyond the physical, an ability shared by adepts and spiritual masters. They can leave the physical body and study the invisible components of life. They can read and decipher the reason why certain events have taken place in the life of others. They can read the Akashic records which are a kind of database of the origin and destiny of individuals and events.

Violet is also the ray of theatre and performance. An actor has the ability to lose herself in the character they are playing. They are able to forget themself and assume another personality.

TODAY'S TASK

Take a look at the colours through a prism. Pause and sense which rays attract, and which repel you, if any? On our evolutionary path, we are required to balance each ray. Spend time visualising and breathing in the colour of each ray. Feel what each stands for and see yourself manifesting that quality in your life.

EXPERIENCE

I sat down, looked at a prism and meditated on the seven rays. I visualised them around me and focussed on which ones felt comfortable and which didn't. I found it difficult to sense and visualise red and violet. They are the extreme ends of the spectrum. The challenge for me with red is that I am going through a phase of being laid back. I'm not keen on taking action and breaking new ground. It was getting a bit stale. I got the message that I had to get things moving in my life. The violet is associated with creativity. It confirmed for me I was not allowing my creative juices to flow in my work. Doing this exercise has helped me to check in with myself. (David)

DAY 17:

WORLD PEACE BEGINS WITH ME

Whether we realise it or not, our moods and state of mind, have an impact on the rest of the world. It's so easy to think that we are just an individual, and that we don't matter in the grand scheme of things. This raises the question: how often are you able to sense when a friend is having a bad day? Even if they try to hide it from you, you are somehow able to pick up that all is not well.

As discussed earlier, we are vibrating beings. We leave traces of our energy on everything we touch and everywhere we go. Someone may board a bus and sit in the same seat that you sat in earlier. For some reason, they might suddenly feel good, and they won't know why. They were previously in a bad mood because something had happened at work, but your good feelings left a trace on the seat that they picked up on.

Experiments confirm that plants grow better, and people heal quicker if their carer takes a real interest in their wellbeing.

At school I had a teacher who was so attentive and positive- that all of us were inspired to do our best. We didn't want to disappoint her, so we worked hard, and her results were very good.

In the 1990s, a meditation group managed to lower the crime rate in an American city, after they meditated on world peace there.

This is all to do with vibrations and emanations. Peaceful energy dissolves and neutralises the harsher atmospheres. The meditation group even claimed that it just takes 1% of the population in an area, to work on peace, to create a change in the crime rate.

However important meditation is, it isn't always easy to do. It takes a lot of practice. It's hard to keep the brain focused on one thing. However, that's part of the fun. When we do succeed, even just for a few minutes, it is so satisfying!

We are all linked on a subtle level, and so our inner state impacts others. We may affect someone we have never met, someone on the other side of the globe. Quantum physics is increasingly finding that this could be the case. Seers tell us that there is an atom in our hearts, that records the movie of our life. It records everything from birth to death! We watch this with our mentors when we leave the earth plane. From this detached vantage point, we can judge ourselves. There is no external Deity judging us. It is our true self that judges our behaviour. Even on a day to day level, we know that even if we try to hide our feelings from friends and family, they can usually pick up on what is truly going on in our world.

TODAY'S TASK

When you sit down to meditate, focus on the cells in your body—your inhabitants. Starting at your feet and working your way up your body, literally let go. Imagine that you are not holding on to anything, that you are allowing your worries to dissolve and disappear, that there is a new freshness to your cells. Once you have done this, focus on your emotions. Are you angry, sad, happy? Let go of any resentment or negativity. Forgive and forget if necessary. Become peaceful and loving.

How about your mind? Are you preoccupied? Leave all your worries for now. You can always come back to them later if you must! Become as mindful and aware as you can. Once you are physically, emotionally, and mentally comfortable you can begin to imagine the world living in peace and harmony, all the countries of the planet working together for the good of the world. Humanity finally realising that we are all interrelated. Soak yourself in the good feelings you experience and enjoy them.

EXPERIENCE

I love doing this meditation for world peace. It can be a challenge, when I have a lot on my mind, and my thoughts keep wandering. But, as they say, practice makes perfect. Eventually I get there and manage to be entirely focussed on peace. This can take time and each day is different, but I usually end up so peaceful. It's a great feeling!(Krish)

DAY 18:

TOUCHING WORLD LEADERS

We live in tempestuous times. Most of the countries in the world are politically polarised. Right or left, conservative or socialist... Certain factions in a country might want independence while others don't.

When someone is elected leader of a country, they then may find that they become the butt of many cruel jokes. Comedians enjoy making jokes about leaders and politicians. They are criticised and ridiculed and sometimes even have to be physically protected to avoid being attacked.

On an energetic level our leaders have to deal with a lot of negativity. They certainly have their fans, but they are also perceived negatively by others. If they are quite sensitive, they can be thrown off- balance by the power of this negative energy. It can then impact how they govern and the destiny of the country itself.

During a recent election in the UK, I found it difficult not to pick a side. After all, I did have to choose a party to vote for. I had to pick the person who I thought had the interests of the whole country at heart. However, if my chosen candidate did not win, (which is what happened), I then had to try to imagine and expect the best future with the new leader. I imagined him making decisions for the good of the country and I learned to send the best thoughts to him. It wasn't easy, but I got there in the end.

TODAY'S TASK

Focus on the leader of your country and, send them the best thoughts and pure light. See them in your imagination working for the good of your country and the world. Even if you don't approve of their ideas politically, by doing this you help them and yourself on a deep level. Visualise other world leaders and sense their light, their true Selves. This exercise neutralises the negative energy that they are receiving from those who don't support them. By sending them clear, pure energy, they are more likely to be inspired and make better decisions for the country.

DAY 19:

CRYSTAL STONED

Natural crystals are formed by the earth's temperature and pressure and they are dug out of the ground. I most frequently use clear quartz crystal and would recommend them to start with. Crystals have been used by humanity for thousands of years. Many religions still incorporate them in their practices today.

Clear quartz crystal has been extolled for its beauty and used as an aid by spiritual groups for thousands of years. It very much reminds us of our potential. It has withstood tough times and a high temperature and emerges beautiful and precious. When we arrive on earth, we have come to learn lessons. Life on earth can be tough but as long as we learn from our mistakes, we are not going to be able to create beauty in our life.

The clear quartz crystal can be a reminder of clarity on all levels: clarity of mind, and purity of emotion and physical health.

Whilst scientists have not been able to find evidence that crystals impact us, they nevertheless accept, that there must be an effect at least on the level of the placebo. When drugs are being tested, the experimenters are obliged to use placebo pills which look similar to the new drug but are just made of sugar. They find that the recipients, often get a positive outcome from them because they believe that the sugar pills are the real thing.

If you believe that working with a crystal is going to help, it will. I consider crystals to be intelligent entities that we can collaborate with to help us with our inner work. If you try what I suggest, you can verify this for yourself.

TODAY'S TASK

This is quite simple. Choose a clear quartz crystal that you find attractive. Run it under cold water, mentally imagining you are cleaning it out. Next, ask the crystal to help you with whatever quality you might be looking to develop. If you are someone who wants to reach your full potential, you might ask it to support you in developing purity and clarity, because these characteristics attract whatever we need in our lives. It can help attract creative ideas, peaceful emotions, and health. You couldn't ask for more!

EXPERIENCE

I began to feel like I had more support in life with my new crystal. It was as if there were an energy working with me to help me reach my goal. It was very heartening. I made sure to wash the crystal and put it in the sun for a few hours, every few days, to cleanse and release all the negative energy which had built up in it. (Lata)

DAY 20:

SOUND IMPACTS OUR LIFE

The health benefits of listening to music are substantial. If you also practice meditation this can be a useful, life-changing and life-enhancing habit. In 2016, Kim Innes, a Professor of Epidemiology, found that music can boost mood and wellbeing. She felt that it had a positive impact on those with insomnia, helping them to fall asleep more easily when coupled with meditation.

Neurologist, Michael Schneck, has found that listening to classical music, lowers blood pressure, and may boost the effectiveness of our inner work as our body is much more relaxed and receptive.

Certain types of music enhance visualisation work. For example, Pachelbel's Canon, helps us reach a quiet space where we can focus thoughts and direct our consciousness more easily. It is these slower beats, known as Adagios, that have a de-stressing impact.

If you listen to a piece of music that you find relaxing and if you are able to re-listen to it without getting bored, you programme your body, to associate it with relaxation. It enters your subconscious mind, and if you are going through a tough time, you just have to listen to that piece to feel less perturbed.

TODAY'S TASK

Find your favourite music, preferably one with an Adagio beat. Create a 'special place' in your imagination, where you feel comfortable and safe. See it in your mind's eye and feel the peace it creates in your body. Make it as vivid and heart- felt as you can, really feel it deeply. The special place you go to with this music, will become more meaningful and profound. With practice it becomes a place where you make discoveries and find peace and solace.

DAY 21:

KINGDOMS OF NATURE

As human beings, we often forget that we share the planet with other natural kingdoms. Our evolution as a species is very dependent on our relationship with these kingdoms.

According to esoteric teachings, we have already worked through the mineral, vegetable and animal kingdoms to reach our human stage. Our evolution as human beings is dependent on how we work with the other kingdoms.

The mineral kingdom, the first kingdom in nature, enhances stability and a sense of being grounded and linked to Mother Earth. If we find that we are getting too cerebral, a walk in nature will ground us and help us feel more balanced.

The vegetable kingdom is less static than the mineral kingdom. Plants are constantly reaching for the sun, and they represent a source of food and air. Many animals are completely vegetarian and rely on plants for their survival. Humans depend on them for nutrition and respiration. We can all see the impact that deforestation is having on the climate and how it's affecting our quality of life.

It takes incarnations to make the leap from the animal to the human kingdom. This happens after an animal's consciousness expands beyond its limits. We see this development especially in more domesticated animals that sometimes behave heroically and protect and help humans. The human kingdom itself is where we all go through evolutionary growth in consciousness, from the selfish to the selfless. So we incarnate in different countries, different races and classes learning and growing and expanding our consciousness. As we evolve, we become more and more aware of our interdependence with the other kingdoms in nature and do our best to live as harmlessly as possible.

TODAY'S TASK

We are going to expand our consciousness to include all the kingdoms in nature. Although we are already linked on the unconscious level, by becoming more conscious of our interconnectedness, we will grow in awareness and our attitude will have a salutary impact on the kingdoms around us.

Throughout the day, sense, and feel your connection to the different kingdoms by choosing a representative for each one. You can imagine a crystal, to represent the mineral kingdom, its clarity and its strength. Perhaps a rose for the vegetable kingdom?

Maybe the patience of an elephant or the wisdom of an owl for the animal kingdom? For the human kingdom, you can choose a 'Godman or woman' who has expanded their consciousness to such a degree that they are at one with the universe.

By remembering our link to the five kingdoms, we are reminding ourselves of our link and interconnectedness to all that lives.

EXPERIENCE

What an eye opener it was for me to begin to feel my link with the other kingdoms. It takes a lot of practice, to hold on to this awareness and it does come and go, but the moments of unity achieved created much wholeness and balance. (Duncan)

DAY 22:

SCREEN TIME

Life before mobile phones was very different. Phones can certainly save so much time and give us access to a whole new world of information and entertainment. But they can also be addictive and time consuming. Look at people in a public place; almost everyone instinctively glances at their phone, as if they are following a strange modern ritual.

During my school and university days, research on any subject involved countless hours spent in the library, looking up information in different books. Today, we just Google a subject to find websites with huge amounts of pertinent information.

Apart from our mobile phones, there are many other screens we look at throughout the day. Our work life inevitably involves screen time, then after work there are more screens: TVs, movies, games etc.

There are the inevitable drawbacks to all this screen time. This sedentary lifestyle can lead to obesity, neck and back pain, as well as weak posture. Then the blue light from TVs, laptops, computers, and mobile phones can affect our sleep. The production of melatonin, the hormone that helps us to fall asleep, is reduced by blue light. Lack of sleep inevitably leads to all kinds of health issues. This is a vicious circle.

Looking at lots of screens may also reduce our creativity and our power of imagination, not to mention our ability to sense the subtle world. The constant barrage of sound and visual entertainment overstimulates us and hinders our ability to hear the quiet voice of intuition.

TODAY'S TASK

Limit the amount of time you spend looking at screens. Choose to go for a walk or spend more time with friends. Start a new hobby or return to one you used to enjoy.

EXPERIENCE

I decided not to take my mobile phone with me when I went out. It was very strange. I kept feeling that I'd forgotten something. I kept touching my pocket absentmindedly. It took me a good while to relax and forget about it. In a strange way, everything seemed to slow down. I found that I was observant of my surroundings and more focussed. There was a sense of clarity and timelessness I will definitely do it again. (Mary)

DAY 23:

IN THE FLOW

Imagine that you are totally engrossed playing tennis. You are playing a tough match and are totally absorbed, clear minded and focused. At such times, you lose all sense of self, time and place. All that matters is the game at hand.

This is what it means to be in the flow. The psychologist Mihaly Csikszentmihalyi interviewed people from all walks of life, including artists, and sportspeople. They all confirmed that they are at their happiest and most creative when absorbed in this way

It can have a huge impact on our lives. The more moments of flow we enjoy, the more compelling and interesting life becomes. During such moments we lose all sense of ego and ironically become more attractive to others, without even trying!

To reach flow we need to be doing something that we love. The task must not be too easy nor too difficult. We are more likely to enter flow when absorbed in a skill that we have worked and developed previously. There are different levels of flow depending on how absorbed we become. An amateur dancer who has just learned a new dance can get into flow, just as much as a professional who knows her steps.

The expression 'in the flow' reminds us of what it means to swim against the current. Being in the flow simply makes everything easier We are carried along and progress without disruption or obstruction.

TODAY'S TASK

Today is a flow day! Pick something that you enjoy doing and do it without especially trying to get into flow. By not trying and simply enjoying it, you are more likely to experience flow. It comes unannounced and when least expected. It cannot be forced; it will come when the conditions are right: when there is total absorption and enjoyment.

EXPERIENCE

I remember what it was like when I was learning how to drive a car. I had to be aware of where my hands and feet were and what was in front and behind. So much to take in. But once I passed my test, I didn't have to concentrate so much. I remember the time I was on a fairly quiet motorway, all my hand and foot movements were fluid and automatic. I did not have to consciously think about each movement. I felt so at one with the countryside all around me. I was alert and totally absorbed. What a great feeling! (Paul)

DAY 24:

BEYOND APPEARANCES

What happens when you walk down the street? It's as if your senses are being "assaulted". Cars, people, shops, posters, planes all vie for attention. You walk past someone, and you notice what they look like: height, clothes, hair, voice. Your senses are taking in information at lightning speed as you assess people that you pass. Could this person be someone you would like to be friends with?

This can go on all day. When we are at work and meeting friends, there is a constant dialogue going on in our heads. We live in a society that extols an analytical approach. Is this a healthy way to live? Well, it is important to notice what's going on around us. In fact, certain jobs rely on an analytical ability, but it's not healthy to be analytical at all times.

The drawback to living this way is that we miss out on the more subtle, powerful side of life. If we want to boost the quality of our life, and have an influence on how it unfurls, we must balance our analytical side with our calmer side.

If we can enjoy being absorbed in the moment, and just being aware, mindful, and watchful, something amazing happens. We become far more intuitive. We just **know** information and synchronicity begins to play a huge part in our life. We seem to be in the right place at the right time.

When we have moments of just being, we experience a new sense of aliveness. We have more energy and don't get tired so easily. We don't waste our energy on judgemental inner conversations anymore.

TODAY'S TASK

When you walk down the street, refuse to indulge in an analytical inner monologue on those you pass. Keep your mind quiet and be aware without being judgemental. It can be done. It involves a type of silence that listens in an alert way, as if you are waiting to receive information. If a thought flits through your mind, just let it. Observe it but make no attempt to follow it. This takes practice, but it is so valuable. Not only does it free up so much mental space, but it may also improve our physical health. You worry so much less, and your stress levels reduce significantly.

EXPERIENCE

I found this exercise tough. It's so hard to stop having an analytical brain. It's difficult not to analyse what someone is wearing or what their appearance is like. There's information coming from all sides, from shops, vehicles, cycles, and cyclists. It took a lot of practice before I began to experience moments of quietness. Moments of attentive awareness were rare, but the more this happened, the more content and less judgmental I became. (Krish)

DAY 25:

CONSCIOUS BREATHING - THE KEY

The act of breathing usually goes unnoticed until something happens. We may notice that we are holding our breath or breathing quickly when we become nervous or angry. Our heart beats faster and we find ourselves in fight or flight mode. The sympathetic nervous system goes on at full throttle.

Breathing is the only system in the body that is both automatic and also subject to control. The link between the mind and breathing is easy to see. Think of a difficult experience you have had, and if you relive it, you will notice how it impacts your breathing, posture and demeanour.

Countless studies confirm that breath-work impacts our health and wellbeing, and just as our inner state has an influence on our breathing, we can breathe in such a way that it influences how we feel.

Awareness of our breathing is crucial if we want to master the thoughts and emotions that we experience. Real change can only take place once our breathing and thought patterns are synchronised and working together to mould consciousness.

All is not lost. The brain, we are told, is constantly rebuilding, and renewing itself. New cells appear and replace the older, less healthy ones. The new cells will mimic the memory and programming of the previous cells. That's why it's hard to change. Our cells are pre-programmed by thoughts and emotions from the past. It is only when we make a concerted effort to re-educate them, and envisage different possibilities, that we witness change in our lives.

Awareness of our breathing is crucial if we want to be aware of the thoughts and emotions that cross our minds. Real change can only take place once our breathing and thought patterns are synchronised and working together to mould consciousness.

TODAY'S TASK

Spend time watching your breathing. Notice how it changes depending on your emotional life. Are you breathing deeply and calmly? Gradually deepen your breath. By doing this, you can encourage your body to relax. This relaxation has countless health benefits.

EXPERIENCE

Whenever I have to do a presentation, my heart beats furiously. My breathing becomes laboured, and I struggle to speak. My voice breaks, and I wish I were elsewhere. Once I learned how to breathe into my Hara centre, things changed dramatically. I felt much more grounded and stable, and my breathing deepened. I was much more confident. (Dan)

DAY 26:

MANTRA MAGIC

A mantra is a word formula that can impact our world. Hindus repeat Sanskrit words that are said to create change. The mantra, when spoken with intensity and fervour, is powerful. It can be said out loud or internally, but sound vibrations impact matter and can even shatter glass. So, if we want to change things in our world, then we can impact the physical plane by saying the mantra out loud.

You can see this when you witness congregations in church saying prayers. The participants are focussed, and you can feel transformations taking place on various levels. Indeed, some congregations witness truly astonishing healing.

Scientific research suggests that mantras can improve and enhance physical, emotional, and mental health. Just spending a few minutes a couple of times a day repeating a mantra can change many things for the better. Whilst chanting a mantra, we inevitably have less opportunity to worry about our daily problems.

For example, the syllable "OM" represents the original sound in Sanskrit. It is said to contain the whole of creation. It is used by Hindus to link with the universe and can be repeated continually to oneself silently or out loud.

TODAY'S TASK

Repeat "OM" to yourself all day as you go about your business. Get a sense of the Absolute, the Universe, the Creator. You can also synchronise your repetition of "OM" with your breathing. Breathe in to the count of four, saying "OM" to yourself as you do so. Then, when you breathe out, say "OM" out loud continuously, until you finish your outbreath. Notice the impact this has when done several times.

DAY 27:

LOVE AS A STATE OF CONSCIOUSNESS

There are many degrees, types, and levels of love. The list is endless: there is love for family, friends, pets, celebrities, nature, countries, etc.

For most, love is of a sexual nature and usually involves "falling" in love. With this type of love, we may feel such a strong attraction to another that we lose control and even pursue them relentlessly.

However, when we talk about love as a state of consciousness, it's not dependent on external circumstances. It's not triggered by a person or an event. It's as if it permeates everyone and everything; a constant stream that flows through and around our world.

Learning how to manifest this love can be a challenge, but when we achieve moments of doing so, it suggests that we have learned to overcome our ego. It also means that we have overcome wanting to be liked by others and shows that the behaviour of others does not influence us. However badly an individual treats us, we are still able to forgive and forget, and hold them in a positive light. It is like an atmosphere that we carry around with us; it touches people, plants, trees, animals, everything that comes within our orbit.

This is the love that spiritual masters manifest after they have spent incarnations and years practising! In the beginning, it is tough. It takes a lot of vigilance and will to manifest love as a state of consciousness for even a few minutes. However, it is the number one lesson we are here to learn, and it is the secret to achieving wisdom and peace of mind. It signifies a crucial step in evolution and signals our ability to overcome significant challenges.

TODAY'S TASK

Send love and kindness to your body. Project a positive energy to all the cells in your feet. Be grateful for all the work they do. Really feel this sense of gratitude, and gradually move up the body: legs, thighs, buttocks, arms, etc. Penetrate your body with loving kindness. Take your time and experience this positive regard for your whole body. Then, move this sense of goodwill beyond yourself. Imagine the space around you, spread this positivity through it, and hold it for as long as you can.

EXPERIENCE

This exercise is a real challenge. I have to consciously stop thinking about my problems. Love as a state of consciousness means manifesting love for no reason, just having a positive regard for all the kingdoms in nature and the people around me. I can only do this for a few minutes before my thinking gets diverted to some other subject. I find that some days it's easier than other days. Surprisingly, though, I have found that throughout the day I'll suddenly and unexpectedly feel joyful for no reason! (Leo)

DAY 28:

BALANCING OUR CENTRES

Our seven major centres are at different points in the etheric body. The etheric body outlines the physical body; they are the sustaining force that keep us well and, if unbalanced, we experience disruption of one kind or another.

We all have our unique strengths and weaknesses. Our spiritual growth depends on our ability to work on ourselves and strengthen our character. Our centres reflect our growth and potential. Clairvoyants tell us that, as we evolve, our spiritual centres reflect this in their sheer beauty of colour and symmetry.

The seven major centres are points of entry for different aspects of spirit to manifest in our lives. By keeping these centres in a state of harmony, we can influence our life experiences and impact the world around us. Each centre presides over a particular area in our life and can be worked on through our attempts to rectify any challenges that we face.

First Centre: The First Centre, at the base of the spine, is concerned with how we manage the practicalities of our daily life. It dictates how we negotiate the physical world. Do we mostly live in the head, and find daily challenges difficult? Are we making a living or is it a constant struggle? Do we look after our body, and its nutritional needs? Do we get enough exercise? This centre is associated with the colour red.

Second Centre: This is our emotional centre, located just below the navel. It is linked to all our relationships, as well as our moods and how much control they have over us. It is a great place to help us manifest ideas and give them substance. This is where we can make theory more practical. We can experience an idea, become passionate about it, and so enable it to become a reality. Orange is the colour of this centre.

Third Centre: Found just below the diaphragm, the third centre, the solar plexus centre, is linked to our different levels of Self. This is where our Personality (ego) as well as our Individuality (soul) can manifest. Those larger-than-life characters who attract attention wherever they go are well-developed in this centre, but people who operate from the soul level are not particularly loud and overpowering. They nevertheless attract attention in a more subtle, energetic way. They have a quiet mystery about them that can be very attractive. The major colour for this centre is yellow.

Fourth Centre: The green heart centre is in the middle of our chest. It is where we interact with others in our world. It has a strong link to nature and peaceful living, and those operating from here are inclusive and understanding. They want to help and serve and so are attracted to medical professions, social work, and teaching. This is where we start to move away from seeing the world purely from our own perspective and begin to see the bigger picture of how everything is interdependent and linked.

Fifth Centre: The blue throat centre is to do with communication and the power of sound. It is sometimes called the third ear! This is where we hear the voice of silence: that intuitive voice that quietly guides us.

Sixth Centre: The Third Eye (indigo ray) reveals our ability to imagine and visualise. When we can discipline our thoughts and imagination, this centre opens. Clairvoyants who can see that which is hidden, have learned to look without preconceived notions. In other words, they approach a subject or person without prejudice. They are neutral and do not influence what they are seeing with their personal beliefs or expectations.

This is what Jesus meant when he said: "If your eye is single, your whole body will be filled with light." In other words, if our perception is not tainted by prior conditioning, we are more likely to reach an accurate assessment.

Seventh Centre: The top of the head, (violet ray) is the centre of spirituality and inspiration. It is our link with spirit. This is the centre that comes into play when we merge with our spiritual selves. It is important to keep our feet on the ground when reaching up to (the) spirit. Like a tree that deepens its roots as it grows taller, we must remember that we are here to learn to bring spirit down into our everyday lives.

TODAY'S TASK

Look at the colour spectrum through a prism and, familiarise yourself with the shade and tone of the rays. As you go through the following exercise, remember the shades you saw through the prism. Start by sitting quietly and spending time going through each centre and the corresponding colour. Start with the red ray, and the centre at the base of the spine. See it with your inner eye. Notice how it makes you feel. Is it easy to sense, or are you struggling? Go through all seven centres. Breathe each ray in several times and sense its corresponding centre. When you have gone through all seven, finish by visualising white light all around you.

EXPERIENCE

I enjoyed this very much! I really felt like I was nourishing myself with the different rays. I was able to sense and visualise some colours better than others. When I checked in, I realised that any unease I felt, related to the life lessons of that particular centre, and the challenges they represented. This was a good reminder of the areas that I need to work on. (David)

DAY 29:

STANDING LIKE A TREE

This is a powerful exercise that originates from the practices of Tai Chi and Qigong. It might seem pointless at first, but if you do it regularly and correctly, you will notice a huge increase in your stamina and tranquillity. Some practitioners call Qigong -- 'acupuncture without needles', because when we assume this pose, our energy system becomes balanced, and we grow more aware of areas of tension or weakness in the body. It will have an impact on the nervous system and our sense of wellbeing whether done inside or outside.

TODAY'S TASK

Stand with your feet shoulder-width apart and your knees slightly bent. Let your arms hang loose, so there is a space underneath your armpits. Try to keep your legs as relaxed as possible and sense from your navel centre. Allow your weight to drop between your feet equally, relaxing your shoulders, head, and upper body as you breathe deeply and slowly. Tuck your pelvis in and feel your spine lengthen. To begin with, do this for just five minutes but increase the time by a few more minutes each day. Eventually you will be able to stand this way for up to twenty minutes.

There should be no pain in the knees. If there is, you will need to shorten the time holding the pose and perhaps bend your knees less. If the front of your thighs hurt a little, this is a sign that you are benefitting from the exercise. You will also find that your thoughts slow down, and you feel more peaceful generally.

EXPERIENCE

This took some getting used to. At first, I felt like it wasn't doing anything. Then, my attention was drawn to my slightly arthritic hands. They began to throb, and I could feel energetic movements there. When I finished the session, I noticed how painful my thighs were. I now practise every day and experience far less pain. My thoughts have slowed down, but I still feel alert. If I miss a day's practice, my sleep is affected, and I am more lethargic. (Jane)

DAY 30:

SILENCE IS GOLDEN

The goal of all these daily exercises is to experience pure silence eventually. You will create a time when the constant inner dialogue has ceased, and you are experiencing the present moment. You will go about life as usual, but with a new clarity and simplicity. You won't constantly be thinking of what someone said or did, and how you responded. You are in the moment, experiencing life in a new way. Your senses will be heightened, and you will begin to notice minute facial expressions, tones, smells and tastes without attachment or judgement.

To get to this stage is extremely difficult, but once you do, the challenge becomes maintaining it. So, to start with, you might enjoy just a few seconds of pure silence before an idea or a comment triggers thoughts and disturbs your quiet mind. It is important to keep alert, attentive and open because, when we do, we become more receptive to 'the voice of silence,' the inner voice that guides us. This voice is very quiet, and you really have to stop all inner ramblings to hear it. But once we do, we will realise how crucial it is for our evolution.

TODAY'S TASK

Before you start your day, sit quietly and just watch your inner world. Notice if you are holding tension anywhere in your body and try to let go of it. If someone has irritated you, see if you can just release any resentment. Make peace with all, forgive, and forget. To hear the 'voice of silence' we have to reach a stage where we genuinely feel no malice towards anyone. It is truly worth the effort.

EXPERIENCE

This has got to be the most difficult exercise. I can only get to the point where all thoughts cease, when I stop worrying about my everyday stuff and just let go. At times, the silence expands, like an atmosphere, beyond my body and merges with the area around my house and town. It is tough to hold onto. Something inevitably disturbs it, and thoughts start again. However, the sense of expansion is so uplifting that I want to practice this more and more. (Alex)

AFTERWORD

So there you have the 30 days of 'assignments'. As with all things, practice makes perfect. The more my friends and I practice these daily assignments, the deeper our understanding grows. There is something immense and profound in us humans and just doing something like this daily, enables us to plumb the depths of our being. I am definitely a 'work in progress'! I find that life grows ever more fascinating as I see changes in myself and all those around me!

Please let me know how you get on. You can contact me with any questions/observations etc at:

changehappensforyou@gmail.com

RECOMMENDED READING

The Complete Works of Omraam Mikhael Aivanhov

The Infinite Way by Joel Goldsmith

ABOUT THE AUTHOR

Duncan has followed a meditation/spiritual lifestyle for some years. He started a group titled "Making Sense of Metaphysics" where he and a group of friends looked at their inner life and its impact on their lifestyle.